WORK

BY ADE DE BETHUNE

CATHOLIC AUTHORS PRESS

MMVII

WORK

Work is man's great vocation. It makes man human. Look at the glory surrounding a "self-made man." He has worked hard; he has "made" himself; we respect him. That he has built up a successful enterprise in a way is not so much what we respect in him as the fact that he has "made" himself. For we all know that the money and the business mean little, and he, also, must leave them behind when he dies. But we respect him because he has built up his character; and that endures beyond death. He has sharpened his intelligence. He has strengthened his will. We respect him because he knows how to work; because he is a man.

Every good workman knows the dignity he attains. He is proud of his good work. He likes it. He is happy with his work. Every skillful, efficient, clever workman is, in fact, much more of a "self-made man" than a mere business man.

He may accumulate no money, but he produces *things* (instead of just exchanging and trading with them). And, in the production of these things, he accumulates, in addition, a wealth of wisdom and self-control and a great joy and pride which make him far happier than money alone ever can. Why? — Because these things endure. Because these are the qualities that make man fully human.

Everyone of us who has been through either war, revolution, inflation or depression of the last 25 years puts no longer much faith in money. It is necessary. But it can't be trusted. Today there is money, and to-morrow it may be lost, confiscated, stolen, or it may have no more buying-power. No shrewd man will put the investment of his entire life on such an undependable thing as money. Wits, ingenuity, resourcefulness are more trustworthy in any emergency. And, since every man desires happiness, and lasting happiness at that, he will be wiser to trust in those things that have a lasting value: in other words, his human faculties. After all is said and done, we must admit that it is only the qualities which a man gains himself that make him a man.

Work is man's great vocation. By working, man is of service to his fellow-man. It is the exalted dignity of labor, that every laborer is doing something useful for his brothers. Every worker who looks at his work from this point of view, suddenly realizes his own value and his own importance. He is a worker. He serves his fellow-men, as they serve him. At his own work, he is a citizen of the world. He is not a parasite, living off plunder, graft, dole or inheritance. He is a worker; he produces goods; he serves mankind.

Men must have sunk very low, before they really prefer a hand-out and slavery to the responsibility and the good pride of work. It is only when they have degenerated, either through enforced misery and idleness or through the soft comfort of money and its idleness, that they lose their humanity and can no longer understand the manly dignity, the real joy of work. Whether professional pan-handlers or idle-rich, they live off taking advantage of their fellow-man. They are cynical softies. Every real worker despises their degradation. It is inhuman. And, because it is inhuman, it is not so common as we might think. Every normal man shrinks from it, and the vast majority of mankind always prefers work, with its dignity and adventure, to a degrading hand-out.

Yet there is a prejudice against work. We all have met it. In fact if we each question ourselves, we will remember having often said: "That's too much work!" or "I don't like to work" or "I wish I had a lot of money, so I wouldn't have to work." We think of work as an evil, a curse, a burden, a drudgery. We try to avoid effort. We hope hopelessly to escape from the necessity of work. Why? Because there is pain and effort in work? — That is no reason to dodge it. Don't we remember that effort makes man? Work brings the triumph of human effort over difficulties.

We all want happiness. But we cannot hope to find it outside of work, for nothing makes man happier than his triumph over difficult problems, even at the cost of suffering. Doesn't a woman, when she is in childbirth, have sorrow, because her hour has come? But when she has brought forth the child, she remembers no longer the anguish, for joy that a man is born into the world. So also there is pain and effort in every work, but that sorrow is turned into joy. The good workman more than forgets his trouble, once he enjoys the triumph of his victory. That indeed makes him a man. We cheat only ourselves by trying to avoid effort.

Ask the workers; they know. Old people will agree with the shipbuilder who remarked one day in a philosophic vein: "People doesn't like to work any more." And he added: "There isn't any of the young fellows what takes pride in his work." As for the old carpenter, he had no illusions: "Them fellows don't want to work," he grunted. "What they want is jobs!" The facts could not be better put. But why don't people like to work? — First, because they think of work as painful. And, especially, because they think of it as degrading.

They want to elevate themselves, to gain culture and refinement — which is good. But they hope to attain this outside of work, enduring to be "laborers" during working hours, so they may have money and leisure to be "gentlemen" at night. They are however fooling themselves. It is impossible to lead this kind of double life. They can never be gentle men on a schedule of just one half of their life. A gentle man is always one, in all his actions.

"Well," they will object, "my work is so uninteresting. How can I like it?" That is very true. Mass-production "jobs" are more than inhuman in their stupefying monotony. No wonder the poor humans must react during leisure moments and forget their slavery in an intoxication of dizzy entertainment. Nothing can be done to alleviate the bestiality of a nerve racking speed-up on the chain-belt. Neither shorter hours, more pay nor more amusements can sugar-coat the slavery of the human beings under the conveyor system. They cannot love their work. It is not work: It is slavery, because the men cannot use their will; they cannot choose to do the work well. And if any there are who pretend differently — who hold out, to a hard-pressed people, freedom from pain and trouble, undisturbed repose and constant enjoyment — they cheat the people and impose upon them, says Pope Leo XIII. And their lying promises will only make the evil worse than before.

Slavery, we hold, must be abolished. It is slavery that degrades man. Not work. We must never despise work. We must never be afraid of it even though work often looks long, painful and tiring, whereas slavery may look more attractive and easy. As a matter of fact there is often little superficial difference between the actions of work and the actions of slavery. The main difference lies in the worker himself. If a man be free, free to work leisurely and well, free to do his job just as he thinks best, no matter what he does, great things or little, it is all "work." And that repays him one hundred per cent, for his effort, in human pride and joy. He needs no leisure and pleasure outside his work. He finds his joy in work. But if that man be a slave, bound either to laziness, cowardice or greed, or (through no fault of his own) to fear, force or starvation, his actions will be marked with the servile spirit of vulgar carelessness, avarice, rush or worry. The result is not work. It is ugly slavery. And the hurried slaves must find an illusion of peace and relaxation elsewhere.

In reaction to the brutalizing slavery of mass-production for profits (not for quality) some people speak of a utopia where all workmen would be happy doing easy and beautiful work. They do not want to make life pleasant by having less work. But they would rather make work itself pleasant. That idea is not bad. It is based on a frank acceptance of work as part of the making of man. It does not try to hide it or avoid it. It just says: "Since work is human, let's have nothing but amusing and agreeable work for everybody." But there is danger in this theory of deluding the public into thinking that every man or woman is, without effort, an accomplished virtuoso, a skillful artist of the hammer or plough or cooking pan. If work were only an easy pastime, this rosy world would exist right now just as ideally satisfying as described.

But the truth of the matter is somewhat different. It is true that work is part of the nature of man, and that it does not pay to sell it into slavery so as to avoid it. It is also very true that every work well done gives the workman a great, filling satisfaction running through his blood. But it must not be forgotten that, because of our fallen nature, work, to be well done, requires great effort, endurance and pain. Work is man's greatest school of life. The most valuable lessons of our life we have learnt only at the cost of the great suffering of work. It was many times worth going through it, and that turns the sorrow into joy. But it never takes away the effort. Only a courageous acceptance of problems, of effort, of suffering, for the sake of the work, will develop a man.

The by-product of work, then, is its being such a useful school for the workman himself. Because every workman knows the discipline of needs and the discipline of materials, because he knows constant effort and constant generosity, he himself is shaped by his work into the dignity of a man. And the only danger that lies at this end, is that many people, earnestly eager to train themselves into self-discipline, for their greater good, use work as a tool for that reason alone. They forget that work brings its legitimate joy. Especially they forget that work is for the service of mankind. Instead they just look upon work as a good suffering, as a healthy discipline, as a busy protection against self-pity and selfishness, as a punishment for sin.

It is true that man is ignorant, forgetful and weak. And it is true that his ignorance, his forgetfulness and his weakness make all his work more struggling than if he were born skillful. It is true that this pain and struggle is the punishment he must endure for his ignorance. But work is not pain and struggle alone. Work is not punishment alone. And the "ascetic" puritans who look upon it as such are also depriving themselves of its greatest value.

Work is for production. It is by his work that man produces necessities, goods, or wealth as it is called. The more a man or a nation produces for himself, the less dependent he is. The more he produces, the less he suffers from unsatisfied needs, the more comfortable and wealthy he is. This comfort is truly the reward of the workman. Don't we always think, for instance, of peace and plenty as the reward of peasants who have reaped an abundant crop? And isn't this generous reward one of the greatest incentives to work? It is a very legitimate incentive, for the laborer is worthy of his hire, whether that be his own production itself, or money wages in exchange for it. As effects follow their cause, so it is right and just that the results of labor should belong to him who has labored, says Pope Leo XIII. Production enriches the workman. It enriches the country. It enriches mankind. It makes life fuller. It makes man more human. And the worker stands up in noble happiness. His strong hands speak of labor and power. He knows his dignity. He is a worker, a producer;

he is, in a way, a "creator"; he is made in the image and likeness of God, the great Producer.

On this side, however, there is again danger of abuse. Our productive power makes us indeed be "little gods." But production is not an end in itself. Nor is the incentive of a reward the true purpose of production. Work has been boosted and placed in a false position. Both the followers of Stalin and those of Ford, in their different ways, have created a veritable worship of production for its own sake: "production for production" and "production for profits," in a mad increase, heading at last into the bitter fallacy of "over-production," with its own dark following of unemployment, destitution and starvation. The abuse of production almost makes it into one of the world's greatest useless evils, a veritable hell on earth. By making a religion out of work, by worshipping "production" as God, in blind idolatry, it really debases work from its true divine function.

Production is not for the sake of more production. It is not for the sake of more profits. Production has a higher function. It is for use. It is for service, for the service of men, who are the children of God. That is why we may say that it is for the service of God. Every worker who thinks of his work as a service to his brothers, gains a great joy. In the drudgery of his daily tasks he can see the service that unites man to man. He can see himself as a working link in the great brotherhood of mankind. And when he further thinks of our human brotherhood under the Fatherhood of God, when he thinks of every man as the child of God; then his work attains a truly sacred function. Work is for the service of man; for the service of God in man; it is a holy worship. Work itself is prayer. Work is a gift, a holy sacrifice, offered gladly, in spite of suffering and pain, for the joy of building up the brotherhood unto the measure of the perfect Man.

Work is for production. And production is for service. It is not for "profits" (though profit is its reward). And again work is not for "punishment," neither is it for "fun" (though it does entail effort on the way and it also gives joy in the victory). Work is strictly for service. And the wealth of profitable production is its reward. As for effort and joy, or rather effort turned into joy, it is its by-product. From his very laboring the worker himself derives a great benefit: he goes through the school of suffering that is turned into joy. And that joy no man can take from him.

By his working itself, by his *making* things, the worker himself is also *made* into a better man. For all human beings, created in the image and likeness of God, may be said to be God's material, which He, the Great Worker, shapes and makes into a perfect image of Himself. We can co-operate with God, in His eternal creative work by being good material. And the best way for us to do this is to know about materials: our own materials in our own work. In fact we can be sure that the degree of our good will at our own daily tasks is also the degree of God's Work in us.

Whenever we work lovingly and well (regardless of the importance or smallness of the work) we have chosen to work well. Whenever we have chosen the good — rather than the less good — we have directed our will towards the Good. Whenever we have followed this direction towards the good, we have followed in fact the direction of the Holy Spirit of God (who therefore is dwelling in us more really). Because God, the great Laborer, works perfectly, whenever we work well, we work especially as He works. Then only can we be transformed into the same image from glory to glory, as by the Spirit of the Lord.

It is our common lot, as men, to work day and night, all our life. We can make this labor be very valuable if we remember always: first that we are working for our brothers, the children of God, and secondly, that we work like God when we work well. Then we will be already (whether at home, factory, school, fields or shop) as the elect in heaven who serve God day and night in His temple.

We want to become good workmen. How can we do this? How can we apply this to our daily life and our ordinary work? — Our success depends, on one hand, upon knowing our materials, and on the other hand upon acquiring our skill, forming our ideas and loving our service. We shall study each one of those in particular that we may then be zealous to accomplish every good work with care and a ready will. For the Lord of all Himself is a Craftsman and he rejoices in His Works.

RAW MATTER

Before the workman stands his raw-matter. She is rough and unshaped and quite meaningless. But she is going to become a "thing" — something for the service of mankind. The workman and his material are starting off on a great adventure together. They must be friends, for they are going to co-operate on a great work. The laborer will give his power and his ideas. The material will contribute the whole of her substance, to be cut, polished and assembled by him. They will work together, hand in hand, the worker and his material, so that the raw-matter will be as it were reborn into a new life.

Who would have thought, seeing my sister's old dresses, all taken apart, that she would have been able to make them into new ones for her little girl? Who would have thought, seeing the odd, dusty pieces of wood, lying here and there, that they could ever have been made, by the carpenter, into an armchair, or by the carver into a graceful statue? The material is still the same, actually no better than before. But she has received from the worker a new form and a new life. This work however, being a co-operative enterprise, depends for its success or unsuccess upon the relations of the worker and the material to one another. How can they be friends to one another for mutual help and mutual good in their great work together? — They must learn to know and trust each other, so they will bring out the best each has to give in the partnership.

To begin with: what are the duties of the workman towards his material? — He must know the material fully before he can shape her successfully. He must know both her possibilities and her limitations. Even the best and most cooperative material cannot do the things outside of her own scope. Only a fool would, for instance, expect to make a boat out of marble or a stove out of wood. Even the best marble will sink and the hardest wood will burn. Do these examples sound crazy? — They are not crazier than our constant efforts at working against our material, as though an enemy, instead of working with and within her limitations.

Haven't we all seen, with our own eyes, countless monstrous aberrations as, for instance, living-room stoves, made of metal, but with a "walnut finish exterior" (for the sake of "dignity" or "beauty" perhaps?). Or frame-houses covered with "imitation brick" shingles? Or steel and concrete sky scrapers covered with "imitation marble" slabs? Or an honest wooden floor painted to fake marble? Our bourgeois age seems to have gone to the limit in producing five-and-ten cent articles that are meant to look like a million dollars. The amount of showy tinsel and cheap "ersatz" that is turned out for every possible product is inconceivable. Is this an age of lies?—of dissimulations? Is it not the mark of those people who always try to play the part of someone outside themselves: a millionaire, a debutante, a movie star, Emily Post or just the Joneses with whom they try so desperately to keep-up? They would be far more successful (and happy) if they took themselves honestly as they are, forgot their romantic dreamings and lived with humility and joy within their income.

Every honest workman knows this well, and he takes each material for what she has to give. The result besides honesty is beauty, because ordinary materials, used with friendship and intelligence by the worker, have their own beauty, sometimes greater than that of costly materials. The good worker loves the poor and the lowly as well as the clever or the rich. He does not despise or hide any under a false mask.

It is the antagonistic sculptor who says: "I will make the marble do what *I* will!" as he imposes with violence an unsuitable shape upon his innocent marble. And the form is liable to be so un-marble-like that ugly looking props are needed to uphold the stone arms and legs. There are certain things that marble cannot do. It is brutal and vulgar to ask them of it, thus going against the laws of Nature. But there are, on the other hand, many useful things that marble can do beautifully when treated with kindness and ingenuity by the worker.

Human material, just as wood, stone and all other materials, also has definite limitations. No man can change human nature (though it can also be glorified into a new life) and it is more than childish to expect of men that they be automatic robots, fitting neatly into a perfectly working State. That is the reason for the distrust we often have of all utopias. They cannot work, we feel, because, pretty as they may be on paper, they are opposed to the nature of the very men for whom they are meant. Let any leader of men use, instead, the human qualities themselves that he finds within the nature of his men, as they really are, and a perfect society will follow.

The workman knows, from his daily experience, that he finds greater freedom by narrowing himself down, voluntarily, to the limitations of his material. Within the limitations themselves, there opens up a vast, an endless field of rich variations and unsuspected possibilities. Those who always work against limitations, have no idea of the freedom and the fun they are missing. They are the prisoners of their own pride. Within the law is liberty.

As men, we, also, are raw matter. When working upon ourselves, improving and making ourselves, it is our first duty to take full stock of both our capacities and our limitations. — "Know thyself." — Then we can really co-operate with our nature instead of having to fight against it; and our potential qualities will have a chance to be glorified into the resplendence of the finished work.

What now are the duties of the material? Or, rather; what are her qualities? For unthinking matter is of course not responsible. It is, in fact, the worker himself who chooses his raw-matter for her qualities. So we can ask him directly: "with what kind of material do you like to work?"

In the first place, every good workman likes clean, fresh and unspoilt material. Especially, however, he requires of his material to be firm, but not to resist his action. How can he work well, on one hand, with cheap, limp stuff that has no body, no backbone, no guts, an indifferent jellyfish? Or, on the other hand, how can he work at all with snobbish, unbending material, that is cussed or stubborn or balks at being worked on and gives no co-operation? Can't we hear the grumbling dressmaker, with her mouth full of pins, who is forced by an indiscriminate customer to use cheap material? She tries and tries to drape it. But it just won't fall gracefully. She tries again this way and that, but there is little she can do. The cheap stuff remains awkward and stiff and rattles noisily as paper. Of course she will do the best she can, but it won't be fun, and no one can expect a really good job with a recalcitrant material.

What then is it that makes good material? How can one tell best quality wool? — or good, ripe apples? — It is something hard to describe, but that a workman knows well: a quality of being soft as well as firm. The material should not resist stubbornly (to the knitting or the eating) neither should she give in weakly. All good knitters and all good apple eaters know this quality instinctively; they need not be told. They like their material supple and strong.

Man makes nothing that does not serve him. So that, as soon as anything is made, out of raw-matter, it serves immediately as a tool for another kind of work. After a cutler, for instance, has finished assembling a pair of scissors, he thinks of it as the end of the work. But the scissors are only just beginning a long and useful new life as the tool of the tailor. And the tailor, when he has sewn the last button and taken out the last thread, says good bye to the clothes on which he has been working. But the clothes, being now finished, are starting off on their own career: they are now the tool of the well-dressed man. Likewise we may say that words are the *material* of the author who shapes them into sentences. And, once shaped, they become the *tools* of the reader at his work of reading. The raw-matter then, becomes a tool, so she can shape some other matter in turn. And, since tools, just as materials, are chosen by the worker for their qualities, we can ask him also: "With what kind of tools do you like to work?"

No worker likes to use dull tools, in poor condition. No worker likes to hunt high and low for a tool that "hides herself" under a disorderly mess. No worker likes using for one job the tool that is meant to fit another. But the good workman always chooses the fitting tool for every part of his work. Whether the tools think themselves important or insignificant, he cares little. He chooses just the ones he needs, and he chooses them with discrimination and à propos. If, however, he finds his tool in bad condition, what will he do but grind her down on a hard sharpening stone, to a bright, keen, cutting edge? Or what will he do, if, looking around, he cannot find her at all? He will leave his work and his ninety-nine other tools, to search till he finds this particular one, hidden in a dark, lonely drawer or under a junk-heap.

The worker, we may say, asks no more of his tools than of his materials. They should both be of good quality and in good condition. And all they need to do is to lie on the workbench, in expectant readiness, awaiting for their turn to be chosen and used, and commending themselves into his hands. If they trust him, he will use them for good work.

It is only by letting herself be worked upon that the raw-matter will be fitted for her new function. She must trust the workman. A grain of wheat trusts the sower when dropped into the ground to die. For, unless it dies, it remains by itself alone. But, if it dies, it bears much fruit. Gladly the raw-matter must love her suffering and her death. Her bad-fortune can then become her good-fortune. Doesn't good silk, after "good luck" has woven her, through a long process, rejoice to be cut again, and pinned, and stitched (and scourged, and spat upon, and crucified) in order to be reborn into a single, beautiful robe?

The raw-matter was, in fact, a prisoner in chains. And what prisoner will not be glad to endure any suffering for freedom? She was as stone, groaning in the dark bowels of the earth: "How long is my exile?" The worker is her liberator and her upholder. From the depths, she cried to him for help: "Thy will be done." And he heard her. He was with her in trouble; he extracted her and he glorified her. From the quarry, he will take her and build her into a road, a bridge, a wall or a house. And now, with the other stones, she rejoices: "We shall go into the house of the Lord!"

Now she has become a new thing, with a new function. Now she is an instrument. As a tool, she helps workers: as a road or a bridge, she helps travellers; as a wall, she protects gardeners; as a house, she shelters families. "I have chosen you," says the workman to his tool. And the expectant tool co-operates: "Thy kingdom come."

Now she has given up her old life and she lives a new life. She has received a new name. We no longer call her: "matter." She is *the work*. We no longer call her: "stone"; she is *a house*. We no longer call her: "wool"; she is *a sweater*. We no longer call her: "flour"; she has become *a cake*. And yet we know that the matter is still in her, probably quite unchanged in quality. Why then has she (although remaining herself) changed her name? — To the workman she has cried: "Hallowed be Thy Name." And he himself came to make her into a new thing giving her a new name.

Now she is shaped though not changed. She is formed, though not destroyed. She is glorified within her own existence. She is now *a house,* a definite house, that individual house, distinct in personality from every other house in the world (though not ceasing for one instant to be "of stone"). Just as a woman changes her maiden name to that of her husband, so the matter receives a new name as a consequence of having become a new thing: a masterpiece, a piece of work, a work of art, an artefact (call her as you wish).

This also is the way God deals with those He wills to exalt. He suffers them to be tempted, afflicted and tormented inwardly and outwardly to the limit of their strength, so that He may deify them, that is unite them to Himself in His wisdom. We are His raw-matter. We are the Work of His hands, and the tools of His Work. As living stones He builds us up into a spiritual house: the Holy City, New Jerusalem, prepared as a bride adorned for her husband, possessing the divine glory.

When man has been reshaped and reformed into God's Image, he is made partaker of the divine nature. He is reborn. He is no longer Peter or John or Tom (although remaining Peter, John and Tom). He also receives a new name: the Name of the image: CHRIST. For the dwelling place of God is with men, and His Name shall be upon their foreheads. He shall dwell with them and they shall be His peoples, and God Himself shall be with them. And He shall wipe every tear from their eyes; and death shall be no more, nor shall grief, nor wailing, nor pain be any more; for the former things are passed away. "Behold, I make all things *new*," says the Lord.

IDEAS

The idea is like a project in the workman's mind. He can see it clearly. He knows what he is going to do. But no one else does. No one can know what he has in mind until he says or does it: shaping the words to fit his thought, or his wood, or his stone, according to his plans.

Now we can all understand his thought and see it realized. The material is probably still just the same as before being used, (for instance wood remains wood, even after it is made into furniture). But now it has become a finished object instead of raw matter. And the very matter's existence is glorified, because the image has been imposed upon it. The unity of the image shines through it. We see no longer the matter alone. We now *see* the image, all realized — face to face — which was the mystery of the workman's mind.

If it were not for work there would be no realization of this idea into the matter. It is work that makes dresses from cloth, houses from stone, stories from words. But where did the workman ever get this idea, which he alone knew, of what he was going to do? Where did it come from? How did he think of it? What made him see it? — Necessity, the necessity, the necessity of some "thing" whose service he craved, without which his life was incomplete and more or less unhappy. It is necessity that drove him to figure out some way in which he can give himself this "thing."

All about us there is plenty of raw material common to each one of us: stone, clay, metal, fruit, straw, wood, wool, words, sounds, colors, movements, etc. . . . We can all see them with our eyes: raw-matter. But the workman is busy, trying to find a way of making this material serve his needs. His brow is knit in a puzzle. He closes his eyes. He thinks and figures. And now he sees no longer the material standing in front of him. His mind's eyes "see" the image. He knows! Quickly he rolls up his sleeves and gets to work. The image is going to come to life.

His image is like a plan in the worker's mind. He knows what he is going to do. He can see it very clearly and gets to work. But after a while, he makes a mistake. He realizes something is not right - - - He stops; upset. His image is lost. He does not remember how he had planned to go about it at this point. And now, in front of him is a half-formed material, quite meaningless and ill-proportioned. The spell is broken. Will he ever know how to finish it? "My God, my God, why hast Thou abandoned me?" A stranger walks in, who sees nothing but loose pieces and thinks the whole thing is orderless and crazy. Incredulously he laughs: That will never fit! But, wait, says the worker; give it a chance! It is not finished.

The worker will not give up. He must not look at his poor, loose pieces as did the stranger who could not even imagine how they might ever be arranged. Instead, he will look again inside himself, strengthen the idea of this thing unseen and unborn, and see it in his mind only as it will be when finished. He refuses to believe the disorder his eyes see. With conviction he believes the invisible! He believes in the order that will come when all the parts are united (when the motor is assembled or the dress is stitched). That no other man can see his idea, matters little; he believes it. To him it is really the substance of the thing which he hopes to make; the evidence of what is still unseen. Firmly, he keeps his image in his mind in spite of every disturbance until it has reformed the whole matter.

What a mystery is the forming of a plan, a clear plan in the imagination, clear as a blue-print. A woman, for instance, walks into her kitchen. For a few instants, in silent communion within herself, she contemplates her provisions and her left-overs; and then she quickly figures out a bright scheme for satisfying all her guests. The mystery of her forming this mental plan for a menu is no different (with due proportions) from the mystery of the scientist who, concentrating upon his facts, comes upon a discovery, or even of the eternal truth which the sage has been made capable of contemplating. We are all privileged to know this mystery, for it remains the same whatever the work.

We are bound to have an idea for everything we do. But how is this idea formed in our mind? How can we make our own imagination produce clear, logical, strong images?— Our mind wanders. It follows thoughts as they go aimlessly and land nowhere, scattered, worried, unrelated as captives in exile. We can't think clearly. We are all in a muddle - - - But, let us stop: "Bring back, Lord, all our captives, as the torrents gather in the South" — and our distracted energies start to collect. In this silent recollection, they converge towards their one center till they are evenly concentrated on it. There is but one center, more or less sharply focused, and from the center, all things are easily seen in their proper order. There is no need to seek the idea far and wide. It will be within us. In the simple recollection of our own thoughts it appears: a unity, sudden, vivid and brilliant, clear and commanding . . . and quickly we set to work, to make it live in our material and in our life.

That is why the story is so meaningful of the Chinese artist who was to restore an old painting in an American Museum. As he came from the busy streets he first prepared his brushes, jars, paints, etc. . . neatly on the floor. Then he knelt down, the picture in front of him. For three hours, says the story, he knelt, contemplating his forebears' great work, banishing all distractions. After he had prayed in silence, quickly he took his brushes and color, and, with swift, smooth, sure strokes he restored the old painting in the joyous spirit in which it had been done.

But to reach this clear vision of the work to be done, all distractions must be mercilessly chased away. When sister, who is cooking the dinner, does not keep her mind on her job, she forgets all about having put salt in the carrots — so she salts them very generously all over again. But her brothers are sure to object violently: "The cook is in love!" they shout. No one can concentrate on two jobs at once. It is true that she was probably all concentrated in thinking about "Jimmy," and in planning how she could shape herself to his loveable image. But while she was planning to do this job so well, she has fallen down on the work at hand of feeding hungry brothers.

So it happens most of the time that being recollected in one thought means being distracted in almost every other, just as an absent-minded professor. It is not until the workman (whatever be his occupation) reaches great skill and ease at his work that he can have multiplicity in unity. At first he is like a baby trying to walk. He concentrates so much on holding his precious balance that he has no chance to think where he is going. As for boxes, toys or stones in the way, he doesn't even see them at all. His whole attention given to one thought excludes every other thought. But as soon as he knows how to walk, then he can easily concentrate on where he is going, and how to get there, and what to avoid, and how to do it well, all of it at one thought, or rather "without giving it a thought," as we say.

As the workman then gains greater control over his work his attention on the main thought begins to contain all other thoughts in unity. It is this unity which makes the beautiful integration of a good work of art. For it is *the same* mind which has conceived both the ensemble of the whole work and every one of its individual details. Why is it that work made in that way is more beautiful? — Because it has more being: that is, all the individual parts are in working harmony with the ensemble. The many are all one. They reflect the same idea in simplicity.

When we think then of the whole universe as one great work it seems plain that in the last analysis there can be but one thought, or one image. There is but one truth: All men who see it, see the same truth. It is simple. God is the great Worker. He also has a working idea: His Image, His Word, His Son. He makes man unto His image. And His idea is extended to men. Just as an artist extends his life into the object he makes, so God also extends His life to us (whom He makes) that we may become partners of the Divine Nature.

As long, however, as we are still incomplete, we can know only partially about this great work, and we must still look forward to the invisible City which has the firm foundations, whose Architect and Builder is God. But, when the Work is finished, when what is perfect arrives, and we are made conformable to God's image, then everything partial shall come to an end. For, in this life, we still see as in a mirror, dimly; but, then, face to face! "Now I know partially," says St. Paul; "but then I shall know completely, just as I am completely known."

Every worker is called to contemplation, in his very work. No matter what is his job, he must visualize it. In the first place, he must "see" by faith an invisible form which will become a loaf of bread, a clean floor, a book, a chair or a machine. But secondly, after the piece of work is finished, he needs no longer to imagine it and believe in it as unseen. Now he can actually *see* it and enjoy it. He *sees* it face to face, for it is in front of him. And he knows it; he knows its every detail (even with his eyes closed he could see it). This is his human happiness.

That is why the workers who do not use their head to work well, really fall down on the job; and, what is more, they fall down in their humanity. Their activity is a mere routine, a bestial monotony of movements. Whether they be prevented from using their heads by being made just "hands" in an irresponsible drudgery, or whether they prevent themselves by laziness, convention, or the insidious paralysis of habit, the result is the same: the work is poor. The work is made, yes, and it probably serves its purpose well enough, but it lacks the added beauty which alone the order in the worker's mind could have given it. We all rejoice at specially good wine, or specially well-fitting clothes, a specially good speech or specially well sung music, or a specially kind person. Perhaps we like wine, clothes, speeches, music or people anyway. But their added excellence gives us, the users, an added happiness. It is the stamp of the worker's individual mind which we recognize. It is himself whom we share, even though, in so many cases, the worker himself lived and died long before we were even born.

So every piece of work demands its maker's thought. But a mere hasty thought is not enough, for whenever workers neglect to plan their work logically before starting, they will get in trouble sooner or later. We all know this well! How often haven't we ourselves rushed headlong into thoughtless action . . . and perhaps never finished the work? If only we had taken the time to do our thinking ahead, we would have visualized the whole work, step by step, and made it easy for ourselves. Rushing, buzzing activity is not all there is to good work. Rest and thought make up half of it. Just as listening is half of talking, so the leisure of concentration makes up one half of every work; that is: its plan.

But before we can gather our thoughts into a plan, we must first have thoughts. This is a platitude, you will say. Of course it is. There are people, however, to whom it does not seem so evident. At least, from hearing their talking about being "original" and "expressing themselves," we might infer that all their ideas were born inside their head by some kind of spontaneous generation. Perhaps they also claim to have a lot of energy and perform great labors without ever having eaten a good meal to produce the said energy. But ordinary sense tells us they are deluding themselves. We know well instead, that, from babies at their mother's breast, to grown men, we all need to take in food before we can give out energy.

It would be foolish to pretend that the same thing is not even more the case for our mind. How can we ever hope to give out a well-developed idea, unless we first received it? A good part of our life must be spent just inbibing material for ideas: observing, reading, looking, listening, watching, taking things in and ordering them in our mind. Then, whenever the work calls for it, the material is ready. If it takes us by surprise, if it comes unexpectedly, as it were, in the middle of the night, we are ready. We have oil to burn in our lamps. We can gather from our stock of knowledge and "create" our own ideas.

It is no plagiarism to take our inspiration from the way Mrs. X. bakes her apples and Mrs. Z. browns onions with her beans, and then come home and make better meals. We are not stealing our thoughts from the past, from classic authors or gothic architecture, or from Nature herself, if we just enrich our minds by studying them, and then make up our own fit ideas with a richer mind. Even though the results may happen to be similar, that is no shame, if, by using our head, we have come to the same conclusion. We do not become chickens, tomatoes or pumpkins by eating them. It is only a slavish copy of externals that is a shame and a degradation which makes the very work groan as a lie.

But there are people on the other hand who live to eat instead of eating to live. This fault is at the opposite extreme. Instead of saying, as the "original minds" do, that they never need to eat food or take ideas from the outside, the "gluttons" never think that they have had enough. They are afraid to start spending their energy or their ideas, for fear they will never replace them. So they accumulate excess food and an excess of facts and data, and their body, or their mind, as the case may be, grows so fat and cumbersome that any movement or creative thought becomes almost an impossibility. They also are deluding themselves. It is only by spending generously both energy and ideas that they can ever become strongly active in mind and body.

So it is a great reason, when men, having all the knowledge of work to be done, are too gluttonous, too lazy, too cowardly or afraid of trouble to bring it to life. They know how to do things well, they can envision works to serve mankind, but they will not do them, allowing talents to go to seed. As they are given a gold piece, they hide it in the ground. They are not workers. They are traitors. They are hearers of the word and not doers. Every man sees in his conscience the way of doing best his own work. And the good workman who then carries it out faithfully as best he knows, will be rewarded with a great increase. Because he worked with his gold piece, he now has ten other ones. And the master says: "Well done, good servant. Because thou wast faithful over little things, I shall set thee over much." Our understanding is given us for work.

How then can we direct our mind to create clearer ideas? — By having our thoughts all concentrated on their work, just as the disciples who (the day of Pentecost having come) were *all gathered in one place,* when suddenly a sound came from heaven, like the rush of a mighty wind and it filled the whole house, and they were all filled with the Holy Spirit. Then we also shall see clearly the idea of God's Work, that we may be fellow-workers for the truth. And, as good laborers, we will not give up, in spite of every trouble. But we will cling to the plan until the Work is done, just as Moses who was steadfast in faith as seeing the Invisible. For we must be doers of the Word and not just listeners, thus deluding ourselves.

SKILL

It is difficult for man to do something new and unknown. He is clumsy and slow. He starts at the wrong end and spoils everything. What bitter travail it is for a child to produce a row of "O's" or "I's" on a piece of paper. All the circles are of different sizes and the lines go shaking every which way. Yet, only a few years later, that same person will write with great ease. There is no longer any question of his being worn out with fatigue at the end of a line. In fact he now writes long letters to his friends with great enthusiasm. He has become skillful enough at the work of handwriting so that it is now truly a pleasure (an easy means to a useful end) instead of a burden.

We all admire the beautiful performance of a skillful skater upon the ice. It looks so easy. And, in fact, it is easy. It is entirely natural (second nature, we call it) and pleasant. "He skates as he breathes!" we say. There is no trace of strain and fatigue in his work. Standing up on the narrow skates is no longer difficult for him. As a matter of fact, he would find it really hard to be clumsy and fall. He is a skillful workman. He acts with endurance and full freedom. He has perfect control.

How did he acquire his skill? — "Oh, I've always skated a lot. I liked trying it." He was generous in his efforts. He worked and worked as much as he could — the more the better. It was not easy, and often he fell. But he that perseveres to the end will be saved. So he picked himself up, laughing, each time he had fallen and tried it immediately all over again without false shame. Till now he is so skillful that he never falls any more and he can go on and on forever, it seems, enjoying himself endlessly.

But when we, ordinary mortals, try to do the same thing, we are probably just as clumsy as he was when he started. Oftentimes, however, we fail to persevere courageously as he did, when learning. Stupidly we compare ourselves to the accomplished artist. But it is hopeless. We can never be as good as he is. Our strained attempts, heavy falls, bruised knees and bumped seat are too much! We give it all up as a bad job!

How many times, however, don't we give up by a false sense of pride, simply because we hate for other people to see our incompetence? We want to hide it. So we keep from doing what we cannot do well. Result: we never learn. By giving up, we have thrown away trouble and work. By giving up we have thrown away a chance of becoming skillful, of becoming human. For a worthless bit of wordly respect, we have damned ourselves to the Hell of having to stand, shivering, on the frozen shore, forever envying in our heart the graceful freedom of the skillful skater.

It is true most people can never become as proficient as he is. They did not start as young and, now, they have many other duties and no time for practice. But, at any rate, we can all become better than we are at what we do, or, at least, we must never hope to improve by just sitting around with freezing envy gnawing at our insides. It takes perseverance, good-will and humility to work oneself out of the painful, difficult, discouraging first-stage. But shirking the effort will not help. Only work gives skill.

"Don't you find," said a skilled old carpenter, "that when you start a new work, the first one takes longer? The next ones you do much faster, I found out. It don't matter what it is: small or big job." And that really includes every kind of job, from the work of lacing shoes to the work of prayer, of which Saint John of the Cross says, that it produces, (as its fruit) the knowledge and love of God (by means of meditation and reflection on His things). "Each time this is done," he says, "it is an act. And, as acts often repeated produce habits, so, many acts of loving knowledge, continuously made, beget the habit in due time." Then it is no longer difficult, and the worker, betaking himself to prayer — like a man with water before him — drinks easily, without effort. Then he will soon come, says St. Benedict, "to that perfect love of God which casts out all fear: whereby he will begin to observe without labor, as though naturally and by habit, all those precepts which formerly he did not observe without fear; no longer for fear of hell, but for love of Christ, and through good habit and delight in virtue.

And this will the Lord deign to show forth by the power of His Spirit in His workman, now cleansed from vice and from sin."

But here comes the question: Why is it that so few ever attain to this? — The reason is that, in this marvellous Work, which God Himself begins, too many are weak, shrinking from trouble, unwilling to endure the least discomfort or mortification, or to labor with constant patience. By leaving any job half-done, or by getting-away with as little work as we dare, we may manage to fool our neighbors, our boss, or even our customer, and to think we have fooled God. But we are in reality cheating only our own selves. We are ruthlessly exploiting and depriving ourselves of the liberty and joy of work skillfully done.

For it is skill that gives us ease, freedom and joy. Any amount of skill does; even very little skill, when it is just acquired, when it is the triumph of perseverance over a difficult problem, when it is the result of having done our best in spite of difficulty. No child, for instance, is very skillful. That is because he has neither lived nor worked much so far. He has not yet grown to the full measure of manhood. But all children do sing, dance, draw, act, think, pray, teach, nurse, cook, wash, buy and sell, etc. . . . They all work. Grown-ups call it "play" but in the children's mind it is "work." However by the time they are ten, somehow the spell is broken, and they do none of these things any more. Why? — "They are too self-conscious," we say, and let it go at that.

It is true that, when they were little, the children didn't seem to mind the crudeness of their work. With just a little imagination a laundry basket could do very well as a make-believe boat, and the back yard as the waves of a stormy sea, or a few scratchy lines on a piece of paper, as a man and his cow. But the children do not remain little always. As each one of them grows in age and size, so also his critical faculties grow. He knows Truth better. He knows more facts about boats, seas, cows. When he looks at his work (or at his toys) in the light of his new knowledge he is bitterly disappointed, for all of a sudden he realizes how inadequate and crude his efforts had been. There follows immediately in any healthy mind, a grim determination to ransack the attic for materials to build a better boat, or to hunt for another piece of paper to draw a better cow. The result is (as a reward, on the side) to have triumphed over the difficulty and become more skillful. Now the young workman's skill has caught up with his critical sense. Now he has the joy of looking at his new work and seeing that it is good.

However, before long, he has become more critical. He "knows better." He sees all the flaws in yesterday's masterpiece; and the same question rises: Can he do it? Will he try again? — Or: Is he despairing? And will he give up? As long as he has the determination to try again, his skill will be sure to grow (by the very trying) and he will catch up in ability with his understanding.

But, when a child despairs at this crucial moment, when he gives in to his ignorance and gives up the work, then is the real tragedy. It is death. It is the cessation of growth. Already the child has begun to die. (Since he has reached the "age of reason," he is now capable of deliberation . . . and of surrender.) His body will go on growing to manhood. And his critical sense will grow more acute as he learns more facts, while his skill is left behind to wither away from lack of practice. He will grow up to be a tall young fellow of twenty, let us say, utterly incapable of drawing more than thin, weak, nervous little lines, or of raising his voice to speak out loud, or of sailing a boat, or swimming, or using an axe, or thinking, or praying perhaps. He is still an undeveloped child of ten as far as these works are concerned, not grown, not free, not happy, defeated by his own false shame and cramped by his lack of skill and fear of criticism. Part of his humanity is left out. He is not a complete man.

Suppose, by now that he has grown up, he gradually

comes to realize his lack of development along some lines. He suffers from it, and makes up his mind to start again where he left off ten years ago. It's going to be a very hard enterprise to resume a broken continuity. But it can be done with good will. He must go back first to being a ten-year-old. With humility he must accept making childish trials and mistakes, cutting his fingers and being ridiculous. But, at the price of these very trials, he will very quickly (for he now has more intelligence of things) become skillful. Soon he will have made up for lost time and resumed the growth that should never have been stopped. The unbroken growth would have been easier for him. But, since he did despair and surrender (and we all do, if not in one thing, at least in another) he can still make up, if he will make a great act of courage, repent, confess, go back to his last stopping point and accept his mistakes instead of dodging them.

The good workman must hope. He must keep on trying with patience, in spite of his mistakes and imperfections. Let not his "sinfulness" crush him down. He must hope. And, as he keeps on working, he will keep on becoming skillful. It is his skill which gives him freedom, so, as long as he perseveres in growth, it may be said that his happiness lives forever. He will indeed grow more critical also, becoming aware of further and further imperfections in his work. But let him rejoice instead of losing hope, for his critical sense can be his greatest help. It prevents him from finding permanent satisfaction with his present skill. It prods him on to do better work — at the same time acquiring more skill and further liberty and happiness for himself.

Ask the workers; they know what this means. "I notice that I have more patience now in learning to sew a little bit," wrote a young fellow when he first had to patch his clothes and tried in earnest. "I remember years ago I used to try to sew and I became impatient immediately when I got my fingers all mixed up trying to use the needle. But now I go very slow and get along quite well. This morning I repaired my overcoat which was ripped in several places. I also sewed on a great big button which had come off the front of the coat. While I sewed I was very happy, and God gave me the grace to shed great, big tears of joy for the privilege of working. These are the rare tears of strength to go on living and trying, and they always quiet the tumult in my heart that, at this particular time had become very disturbing to me. These are the same tears that I saw my mother shed many, many times, when I was a little boy, while she was working in the kitchen or washing the dishes or milking the cows. After she had wiped away the tears, she would say to me: 'Son, I wish I was in heaven!' "

Man is not born with skill. He must acquire it through practice. Practice makes perfect. But that means a lot of practice — a lot of work. Those who are afraid of work, will never gain the freedom of skill. Those men are broken with toil even though they be young; the strength of their youth sinks in weakness. But those who hope in the Lord shall renew their strength. They shall soar up on wings like eagles. They shall run and not be weary. They shall walk and not faint. Amid earthly things they lift up their hearts to heaven. For the Lord Himself is a Worker. He created the whole earth and yet His Power never slackens, His Work is never labored, and there is no fathoming the Wisdom He builds with. He gives strength to the weary. He builds up again and again the brawn of those who once were nothing. By His great Power and Strength He Shepherds all His Work. None of it is ever wasted.

SERVICE

Whenever workers are conscious of the value of their work they are happy men. The small craftsman, who works in his own little shop, is in a privileged position in this respect, for he can see, at first hand, how serviceable his products are to his customers. If the customers are satisfied, they come back for more and he has a lively trade. That is why the boss of a larger factory is wise if he keeps all his workers informed all the time where their work is going and what new jobs are coming in. In this way the workers are kept happy, knowing that they are doing good work. The factory is like a large family, and the workers are co-operating in a great common work.

But it is evident that such conditions are impossible in the gigantic offices and plants where the men are numbered as so many machines. No foreman knows them all. They do not even know their neighbor. And especially, as they are always doing the same narrow part of the work, they never see the finished product; and least of all they never see the eventual customers. The workers do not know for whom they are working. They hardly ever know on what they are working or for what they are working. The only assurance left to them is that they are working for money. Because they all know that they need money to live.

And so the idea is held that man works for money. But that idea is false. The good workman does not work for money. Peter Maurin says: "Labor is a gift. It is not a commodity." Peter means that labor cannot be bought or sold on the bargain counter, for the highest or the lowest bid (according to which side of the counter has the most power). Labor can only be given — freely given by a free man. If it be not given, it is slavery: it is sold and bought; it is meaningless and valueless. It is not human.

Labor is a gift. Does that mean to say, however, that no one should be paid for his work? Isn't the laborer worthy of his hire? — Yes. And Peter is the first to claim it. But it is the *laborer* who is worthy of his hire. It is he who needs his hire; but not the *labor*. No one can value the labor or the work itself in other terms than as a free gift. Labor is a gift. But neither does that mean that the poor worker is to offer his productions as a gift to his patron. That would be nonsense.

This rather is the idea: that the laborer offers *himself* as a gift *to his work*. His devotion and his painstaking care are his own gift to his work. It is the gift for which no money, no honors, no bribe can pay. Men can be forced to work (through force or necessity). But no worker can be made to love his work. If it happens that he works specially well, it is because he chooses to do so himself, because he wants to. It is his own free choice as a free human being. His labor is a gift.

Man always loves the ones to whom he gives himself. He also will love his work to the extent to which he puts himself into it. Even though he makes it for another man to use, his work will always be his, because he, in the first place, gave it freely of his time, his skill and his energy. The more whole-heartedly he has given himself to his work, the more intimately the work remains his. Unconsciously we recognize this when we say: "This is a Chippendale chair." We say that, because Chippendale made the chair. He made it, we realize, for Mr. So-and-so. But we no longer know the customer's name after two centuries. We still know the worker's name, however, which shows how really his work was his own, for he had given it so much of himself.

Perhaps it means working early and late and doing without some ease or comfort, for the workman to give himself so generously to his work. But he is really happy to do it for someone for whom he cares: his family, his friends, his friendly customers. He will take special pains when he chooses to; but that is no hard sacrifice, for the human joy of freely giving of his own. To sacrifice himself thus for the good of the work does not make of him a slave. Giving does not make a man less human. Giving is what makes man human. Love is an exchange of gifts. Wherever love exists, it works, and if it is great, it works great things.

It is only when circumstances actually prevent us from working well that we cannot make the gift of ourselves and our enthusiasm to our work. Then indeed we are slaves. But what is it that prevents us from giving it our full time and attention? — Rush and hurry. We may be rushed in cooking the dinner, because of coming home late and wanting to go to the movies afterwards. The dinner will suffer. It won't be very good. No one will be happy, and the chances are that we won't enjoy the movies as well. (As long as it is a necessity for us to eat dinner, why not take the trouble to do *it* well, and enjoy it?) Or we may be rushed through laziness or disorder, or scatter-brained planning of our work, or indecision. Or again we may be rushed by greed, for profits, preferring quantity to quality. Or, on the other hand we may be rushed, through no fault of our own by an exacting and thoughtless customer, or by the boss who wants to speed-up production for his own profits, or by the fear of a threatening mortgage or landlord. In all cases, however, it is the customer who suffers, since he receives a half-cooked dinner or a poorly made merchandise. Now if the customer suffers, justice does. Isn't production for service?

If a man will give his fellow-man a treacherous service, what was the use of doing the work? What was the use of building the city and of keeping it and of rising before daybreak to labor? What will it profit the worker if he produce a lot, but it is of no service? He will be left with his wages in his empty hands, but no happiness.

The free workman knows that his production is for service. His work is his gift to mankind. He controls his work. He has power over it. He may decide to do it or not to do it. He may choose to do it well or badly. It is up to him to pass judgment. He is the one who must choose for instance whether to wear a blue tie or a brown tie, whether to bake an apple pie or a pumpkin pie, whether to take a second helping of potatoes or not, whether to file his records alphabetically or chronologically, whether to write straight or slanting, large or small, whether to close the window or leave it open. No matter how unimportant the work is, someone must decide how it is going to be done. Only a human being can judge and decide. We all do it so automatically in every day matters that we forget to realize it is exactly the same kind of judgment that goes into the creation of the greatest and noblest human works. We all use our will.

The men who do not use their will are cowards. They are afraid to suffer from the consequences of their choice. They are slaves. Those who use their will to choose evil are perverts. And they become the slaves of their own perversion. But the man who uses his will to choose the good (regardless of hardships) is alone, the free man. It is every real worker's privilege that he can use his free will; and, by choosing to do good work well, he can train his own will.

It is the worker's privilege that he is a judge at his work. But that also implies the duty for him to be truly impartial. Because he uses his will does not mean that he may do just what he happens to want. "I am not come to do my will, but the will of him that sent me." And he that sent the workman out to do the work is: the-service-of-his-fellow-man. When he has considered the good of his customer, the good of his work and of every circumstance that bears upon it, in the balance with his own interest, then he can render an impartial sentence. If he follows his just decision, he will never be moved to its detriment by his own ease, comfort or gain, or any bribery. He will do faithfully the work that he judges good. Then he has truly chosen the will of his service to be his own will and he can say: "Not my will be done, but Thy Will."

It is only when men have lost sight of their noble mission as workers that they fall down into the sin of carrying on useless activities for their own self-will. Some men are so savage that they need war, fighting or murder to exercise their desire for struggle and victory. Other barbarians lead such an unnatural life that they need empty physical exercise to keep fit. They rush back and forth from work in trains or cars in order to save time, so they can go and waste their time on a golf course, because they need walking for their health. It is a puritan attitude in both cases. Work is debased to being just discipline and mortification for its own sake. Those men *punish* themselves either with war or with exercise and sterile sport.

On the other hand there are those who think their activity is for pleasure alone. Some abuse their skill just for the fun of showing-off. They display with pride their cleverness in fancy tours-de-force. But isn't everyone bored stiff with a self-satisfied speaker's endless speeches, with a violinist's tricks of virtuosity, or with a temperamental artist's expressions of his sub-conscious? Their work pleases no one but their own little ego. Other people waste their time and energy in social functions, parties, joyless play, vacuous reading — all just "to get a thrilling experience." They give themselves all this trouble just to *amuse* themselves in sterile entertainment or self-indulgence. They work very hard, but no one profits from their barren activity. They also have debased the noble purpose of work. Their deeds have no service; they are of no use — sterile activity, a real waste of time.

Work then is neither for punishment nor for amusement, but for use. In his good work, the laborer finds his own gift to offer to mankind. All production is for use; and that means every conceivable production, for all the needs of man: his body's needs and his mind's needs and his spiritual needs. All men who are dedicated to some human service are doing real work: builders, craftsmen, artisans, artists, manufacturers, makers, producers, operators, actors, travellers, teachers, doctors, peasants, cultivators, laborers, mothers, workers of every kind. All men are called to this great vocation: their priestly office, to offer sacrifice. A sacrifice is a gift. What they offer is the gift of themselves — their power, their intelligence and their devotion — to their work.

All men are called to work. We too. Each one of us in our own life, big or small, every day. If in the counsel of His Will, God has brought us to the beginning of this day,

He will save us (who will salvation) so that we may not turn aside into sin, but, rather, that always our words may be spoken, and our thoughts and works be directed unto the making of His Justice. How then can we fulfill this great function and make — as St. Teresa of Lisieux did — a meaningful act out of every insignificant duty of our life? — By learning to work well for the love of our fellow-man, by learning to take trouble with our work and to enjoy it. No good worker is too proud or too unconcerned to give his time and attention to any work. He is successful and happy because he does even little details carefully. When we sadly envy him his happiness, are we not forgetting that we could do just the same, if we only wanted to?

It is easily within anyone's reach to do his work with care and devotion, especially when he remembers the value of his service to those whom he loves and respects. Whenever the question comes: "Oh, this is good enough! I can let it go at that. Who will know the difference?" the good workman answers: "Well, I can still do it a little better." The stone cutters of the middle ages who carved the incredible capitals in their old cathedrals did not think whether the public should ever see or not see their own work. They carved their stones with as much care and love, even though they were to be placed way up high or in some hidden corner. Dutch housewives also are said to be so clean that the "underneaths" and the "behinds" and the "insides" are just as immaculately clean as the visible parts of their homes.

These are good workers who do their service well. In the exuberance of their devotion they always think of better ways of doing it and of enriching it with the gift of themselves. It is from this generous giving that art is born: the doing of every useful work in a specially beautiful and resplendent way. And this is the added blessing that the good workman brings to the world: not only the happiness of his own good conscience, but also the beauty of his work which we all enjoy.

THE DIGNITY OF LABOR

We agree that work is a necessity. Whether or not we like to admit it, we must face the fact: it is our common lot to work all our life. We may go on living with the dream that sometime we shall escape the necessity of work. But that is only a delusion. As long as we live, there will be work for us to do. So we might as well make up our mind to accept the idea.

For we notice that the leisure of sickness or unemployment, or perhaps money, does not make anyone really happy. Idleness does not take away suffering. So we must come to the conclusion that merely avoiding work, or even trying to escape from suffering, will not make us happy.

Instead we notice the good pride of a conscientious worker, and that is why we cannot help but realize how truly it is our great dignity to work in our life. However it isn't just because of its usefulness to us, that our work is our vocation. Naturally if it were not useful for our needs there would be no work at all. But over and beyond that, it is our great vocation, our pride and our dignity. Why? — Labor is man's use of his own intelligence and his will. The more he uses his intelligence, the more intelligent he becomes. By his own work man is made more human. By his good work every man gains a great nobility. No wonder then that his free labor elevates the worker. No wonder it is such a privilege. Not only does every worker know he is serving mankind but also he is doing a thing similar to what God Himself does in great majesty and power: he works. By his own working, man is made a fellow-worker of God Himself; he shares in God's creative action.

Just as the workman produces all kinds of good things by the power of his hands and his mind and will, so also, long before him, God had made all things by His Labor. We ourselves had to be made by God before we could even do any action whatsoever. So this really is the dignity of our work: that we are made in the image and semblance of God Who works. We are made in His image: fit to know, to love and also to serve. And what is this service of God after all, but our own ordinary work: using our intelligence and our love at our daily tasks?

So, just as we dig ditches and cut wood, cook meals and make clothes, write books, or read them, and do all kinds of work, so also God works even now to make us. Just as man, whom we know, labors on his raw matter, to make it as he wants,

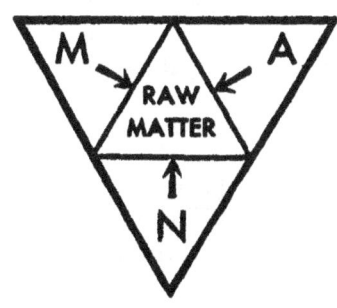

just so does God, Whom we do not know, work on us, His raw matter, to make us partakers of His Divinity.

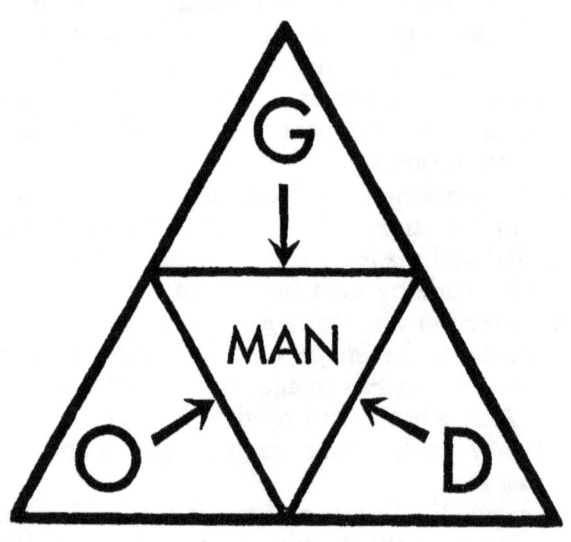

God works on us all the time. Even to this moment He continues His Great Work. Every day He perfects each one of us, with our own willing help. By His power, we are, as it were, "made" to be perfect as our invisible Father is perfect. It is He Who makes us. And yet doesn't it often seem to us that we make ourselves? — Yes, we do ourselves work, says St. Augustine; but we are co-workers with Him Who does the Work.

For God invites us to be His fellow-workers somewhat as a fond Daddy who is building a scooter for his little one, and lets him help too. Perhaps the scooter won't be quite as perfect as it might have been if Daddy had gone out to make it all by himself, without interference. But the little fellow will love it much better because he had his share in making it. (And doesn't the good father desire his child's happiness rather than a dozen perfect scooters?) What are a few crooked nails and rough edges, and a bit of patching up, next to the joy of the little boy who loves the toy he made and will go out scooting on it for days on end?

God then makes a beginning, St. Augustine explains, working in us so that we may have the will. And, in perfecting, He works in us when we have the will. He operates therefore, first, without us, in order that we may will. But as soon as we will (and so will as to act) then He co-operates with us. However we can do nothing to effect good works without Him, either working that we may will, or co-working with us.

We may then truly rejoice: we can and we are free to "make" ourselves. St. Paul himself says plainly: "I have labored more abudantly than they. Yet not I, but the grace of God in me." So it is God who really accomplishes our work. And, after all is said and done, many more valuable things will be produced by our enduring and suffering so He can labor on us, than by any mighty labors we could think of performing ourselves. For, as St. Irenaeus points out, our nature is ultimately a thing *to be made* rather than a thing *that makes*.

"So you, for your part," he adds, "should present your heart soft and pliant and moist, lest you become so hard that you loose the traces of His fingers. And you should keep carefully the shape in which the Artist fashioned you. By preserving carefully the framework you may rise to perfection. For any stain in you will be covered by the Craftsmanship of God. He will make of you a definite thing. His hand will overlay you inside and outside with pure gold and silver. He will make you so good that even the King Himself will desire your beauty.

"But if, instead, you are hardened, you will cast off His Art and become ugly to Him. Since, of your nature, you require to be made, when you displease God, you loose His Art and you loose life. For it belongs to the kind goodness of God *to make*. But it is the nature of man *to be made*.

"If then, you hand over to Him what is yours (that is: faith in Him and subjection) you will take entire possession of His Art, and you will be a perfect Work of God. If, however you have not believed in Him, if you have fled His hand, then the cause of your imperfection will be in you who have not obeyed and not in Him Who calls. The Art of God does not fail. He can raise up from stones children of Abraham. But any man who does not co-operate with that Art, is himself the cause of his own imperfection."

What then is this enduring and this suffering which will allow God to do His valuable work in us? How can we keep our hearts soft and pliant? Shall we just do nothing but sit and wait? "Shall we stop making good things and abandon love?" says St. Clement. "The Lord forbid that this should happen, at least to us! But let us be zealous to accomplish every good work with care and a ready will, for the Lord of all Himself is a Craftsman and He rejoices in His Works." He did not make us for idleness, even though we are finally shaped by His hand.

Ultimately we are *God's material*. And, as such, we need to be soft and pliant as the material to be perfected that seems to lie under the hand of the artist. For we realize our powerlessness to do anything by ourselves alone. But, in the meantime, we are also made to be *human workers*, little gods, who control and shape matter. And we know by necessity that we must labor every day of our life to the end. Which vocation shall we follow? To be the material: enduring? — or the worker: commanding?

The two vocations are only one. We must accept the challenge of our human life of work whether at home or in the fields or the shop or the school or the office or the factory.

Precisely within the responsibility of commanding our own small daily tasks, we shall find the necessity of enduring, of effort, of patient trials, of monotony and countless details demanding attention. This is the discipline of gentle suffering which makes the good worker be soft and pliant under the hands of God. He accepts hardships and long hours of toil, he loves them and chooses them for the good of his work. He is good *divine material* by being a good, responsible, *human worker*.

St. Catherine of Genoa says that God works in us as He wishes, so subtly and secretly that the man in whom the work is being accomplished does not himself perceive it. But, if he should perceive it and if he should bless the Lord and co-operate, would it not be better? But on the other hand how can anyone recognize the craftsmanship of God if this be not visible? Unless the Lord Himself should appear to us and say in plain language: "I am working on you," how shall *we* recognize His hand in our own ordinary life?

He is to be found, not far away and in no extraordinary manner. But He is found working on us at whatever our own life's work may be. Wherever we meet difficulties to overcome, heavy labor to endure, trouble to take, effort to sustain, *there* He also is doing His great work, and we at our very toils are His responsive material. That is the dignity of responsibility and its troubles at our work.

Whatever our occupation then, we can offer the effort of our own good work. It is our own offering, itself transformed into the great everlasting Work of the Creator, in which we share. The very effort of his daily toil which the Christian offers at Mass is also transformed. In each of his different occupations, he can make his work to be the extension of the great Work of the Mass, throughout the day and the night. It is his small offering but which can be transformed and in which all will share.

But only a complete man can produce real human work. Only real human work is worthy to be called "work." Only intelligent and conscientious work combines man's double vocation to contemplation and action. No matter how small and insignificant our work may seem, it is worthy to be done well and to share in this dignity. Whether we build a cathedral, sing beautiful songs and speak immortal words, or whether we open and close doors, lace our shoes, tie up bundles and wash dishes, our work is made up equally of *contemplation* (in seeing the image of what is to be done) and of *action* (in laboring with skill to do it). Our *judgment* throughout directs both, to see and to do what is right.

When, however any work is deprived of its *contemplation* it becomes mere physical labor. The workers who are not able to think responsibly of what they are doing are no more than slaves chained to a meaningless action. When however work is deprived of its *action* it degenerates into the sterile speculation of men who only plan unpractical schemes for underlings to carry out, or else it may degenerate into a real incapacity for thinking itself, a slavish acceptance of all ready-made standards supplied by public-opinion (whether of gossip or a commercialized press, radio or movies).

Both are a form of slavery. But when work is deprived of its impartial *judgment* to direct it, it sinks even lower. It becomes a perversion, an immoral parody, a sacrilegious simulation of the real joy of work. It is the most treacherous way of betraying both work and humanity to do the right deeds for the wrong reason. Perversion is the worst slavery.

Anyone who is free to do a simple work (like eating an apple or sweeping the floor) as a full human being, well and leisurely — creatively, as it is sometimes said — approaches to the complete perfection of God. He approaches it more closely, at his small work than will any worker who is not a complete free man, no matter how lucid a thinker, how skillful an artist or even how disinterested a judge he may happen to be. Perhaps the free workman performs exactly the same actions as the slave — but not in the same spirit. His freedom is not due to the kind of actions he does. Nor is it due entirely to the conditions under which he labors. His freedom comes chiefly from his own attitude of disinterested good will. The highest manifestation of life consists in this: that a being governs his own actions, says St. Thomas Aquinas. A thing which is always subject to the direction of another is somewhat of a dead thing. Now a slave does not govern his own actions, but rather they are governed for him. Hence a man, in so far as he is a slave, is a veritable image of death. We know, it is true, that inhuman conditions render servility so hard to avoid that the poor slaves finally no longer realize there is such a thing as human dignity and free-will. But, in the end, we are bound to admit that men are slaves only when they do not use their human faculties. They allow people and circumstances to drive them. They choose nothing.

But the free workman chooses to do any kind of work as well as he can. He chooses to see the good in any condition. And so he works well and skillfully. He loves the work to which he has given himself, and his free spirit can rise above his condition. Martin de Porres, in 16th century Peru, a Negro despised and abused by all, even his own relatives, chooses to forgive them their snobbishness. He chooses to work as conscientiously as possible at his job tending the sick; cures their infections with great skill; feeds starving prisoners as best he can; adopts homeless children with a father's devotion; and grows so much in holiness that we now think of him as one of the great figures of mankind. In social condition born — and living — no better than a slave. In everlasting spirit a free workman.

So we cannot say that certain actions are work and others slavery (or drudgery). Any action (even the most intellectual or spiritual) is capable of being sold into slavery. Yet there is not a single necessary human duty (no matter how "menial") that should not be fulfilled intelligently and devotedly in a truly humanizing way. Slavery, then, is any activity, carried out carelessly by compulsion of fear, tyranny or starvation; not for use, but for profits; not intelligently but irresponsibly, sub-humanly. But work can be any activity fully undertaken by man, for human needs, in the best intelligent human manner. Any free human work produces Beauty.

The duty of work need not be a crippling burden to man. It is up to him to be intelligent and conscientious about it, so as to make of his labor a way of life that leads to the happiness of God. We shall, therefore, deprive ourselves of the happiness which is our due as long as we hate and try to avoid work which is our duty. For there is nothing so easy, says Terence, but that it becomes difficult when you do it with reluctance. And St. Thomas points out that it belongs to the virtue of magnificence to spend much in order that some great work be accomplished in a becoming manner. Therefore, slaves, servants and machines designed to save us from work (rather than do the work better) really deprive us of the joy of effort, and we are wise to flee them as poison. But we must instead equip ourselves with all the help, the tools and the machinery that will contribute to doing better work, no matter what trouble it will entail. The trouble will become a rewarding joy.

It is natural for anyone to love his work, says St. Thomas Aquinas, and this is so because each one loves his existence and life, which is manifested chiefly in his activity. A good work, moreover, affords greater joy, says St. Augustine, in proportion as God is more and more loved as the supreme and immutable Good, and as the Author of all good things of every kind whatever. No matter then what is our occupation, it is worthy to be done well, with our full humanity fully offered for service. The joy of the ultimate contemplation is already our reward when we can see our beautiful work all finished. Everyone of our works can equally bear the joyous stamp of our humanity. For no action is worthless, and the fullness of God is worthy to be glorified in all things.

www.ingramcontent.com/pod-product-compliance
Lightning Source LLC
Chambersburg PA
CBHW031437040426
42444CB00006B/852